Jean-Pierre Filiu & David B.

BEST OF ENEMIES

A History of US and Middle East Relations

Part Two: 1953-1984

First published in English in 2014
by SelfMadeHero
139–141 Pancras Road
London NWI IUN
www.selfmadehero.com

English translation © 2014 SelfMadeHero

Written by: Jean-Pierre Filiu and David B.
Illustrated by: David B.
Translated from the French edition by Edward Gauvin

Publishing Assistant: Guillaume Rater
Editorial & Production Manager: Lizzie Kaye
Sales & Marketing Manager: Sam Humphrey
Publishing Director: Emma Hayley
With thanks to: Nick de Somogyi and Jane Laporte
David B. font provided by Coconino Press

First published in French by Futuropolis in 2014
© Futuropolis, Paris, 2014

All rights reserved. No portion of this book may be reproduced,
stored in a retrieval system, or transmitted in any form or by
any means, mechanical, electronic, photocopying, recording,
or otherwise, without written permission from the publisher.

A CIP record for this book is available from the British Library

ISBN: 978-1-906838-84-3

10 9 8 7 6 5 4 3 2 1

Printed and bound in China

Jean-Pierre Filiu & David B.

BEST OF ENEMIES

A History of US and Middle East Relations

Part Two: 1953-1984

SELF MADE HERO

5 Six Days

In the 1950s, the Middle East only interested the U.S. in the context of the Cold War, which was getting perilously hot in certain spots around the world.

President Eisenhower was afraid of seeing another Korean War break out in the East.

Soviet intervention in Hungary alarmed him.

This drove him to put a sharp check on the Franco-British-Israeli offensive against Nasser in 1956.

But the president's grand gesture to save Nasser's regime from military defeat contradicted his own actions.

As early as March 1956, he had secretly adopted the "Omega" plan.

This plan aimed to isolate Egypt by cozying up to Saudi Arabia, where King Saud was succeeding Ibn Saud.

In 1957, Eisenhower gave a bellicose speech with warlike overtones to Congress.

Russia's rulers have long sought to dominate the Middle East. That was true of the Czars and it is true of the Bolsheviks.

The "Eisenhower Doctrine" was absolutely uncompromising toward alleged ties between Moscow and the Middle East.

The Soviet rulers continue to show that they do not scruple to use any means to gain their ends.

The free nations of the Middle East need, and for the most part want, added strength to assure their continued independence.

Shortly after this speech, King Saud came to D.C. on an official visit, where he was welcomed with pomp and splendor.

The U.S. financed highways to Mecca and Medina.

Making the Hajj easier for pilgrims enhanced the religious prestige of the Wahhabi dynasty.

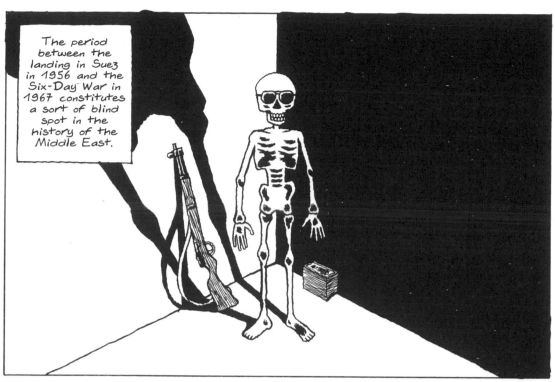

The period between the landing in Suez in 1956 and the Six-Day War in 1967 constitutes a sort of blind spot in the history of the Middle East.

King Hussein of Jordan adopted an anti-Nasser stance.

In April 1957, he dismissed the nationalist government.

The U.S. sent a fleet to the Mediterranean to support the king.

Boosted by this support, the king proclaimed martial law, dissolved political parties, and drove out the pro-Nasserites.

In Syria, Kermit Roosevelt used every means at his disposal to subvert the nationalist regime.

But his ventures failed, and many American "diplomats" were expelled from Damascus.

On 1 February 1958, the United Arab Republic, born of a union between Syria and Egypt, was declared.

But conflicts arose; Cairo treated its northern province like a proconsulate, a gift to its own liege lords.

In July, revolutionaries led by General Kassem seized power in Iraq and massacred the royal family.

Egyptian hegemony spread in the region.

The English-speaking world reacted immediately. The British government sent paratroopers to Amman to protect King Hussein.

American marines landed on the beach at Beirut to save Lebanon from Nasser's clutches.

All they found were bewildered sunbathers.

In Cairo, the message was received loud and clear. Nasser hastened to placate the Americans.

Communists were viciously suppressed.

In Iraq, however, General Kassem used communist militia to suppress the pro-Nasser uprising in the city of Mosul.

January 1961 saw J.F.K.'s inauguration. His support for Algerian independence had made him very popular in Egypt, and throughout the Arab world.

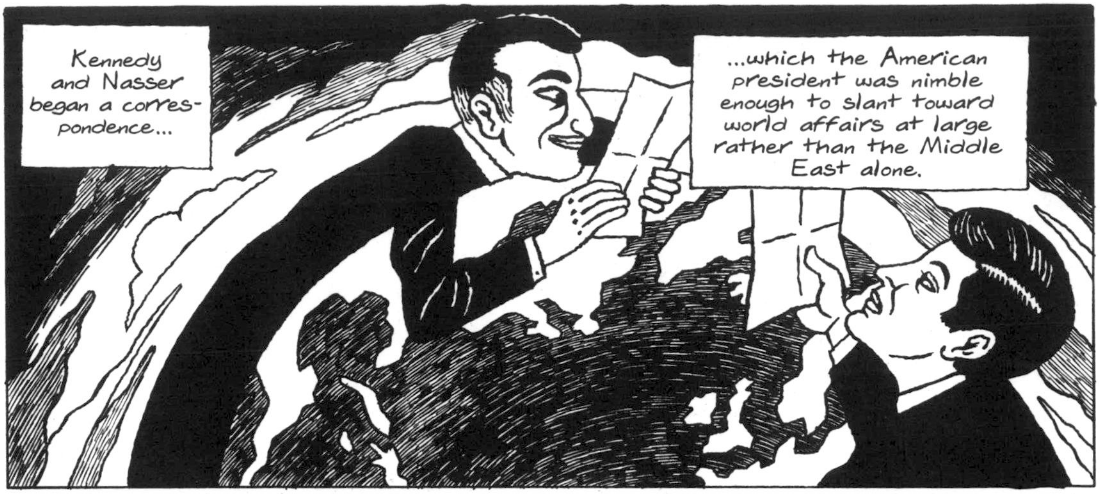
Kennedy and Nasser began a corres- pondence...
...which the American president was nimble enough to slant toward world affairs at large rather than the Middle East alone.

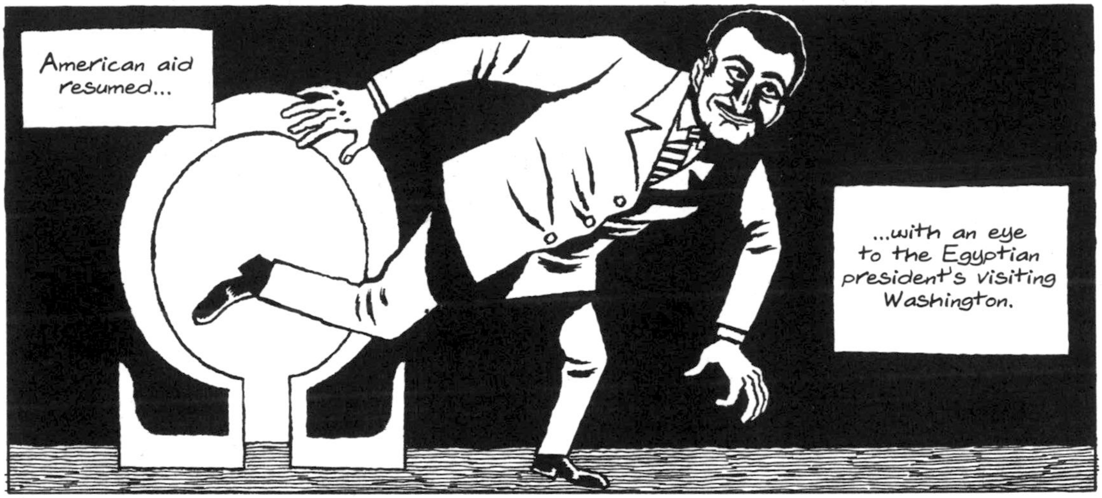
American aid resumed...
...with an eye to the Egyptian president's visiting Washington.

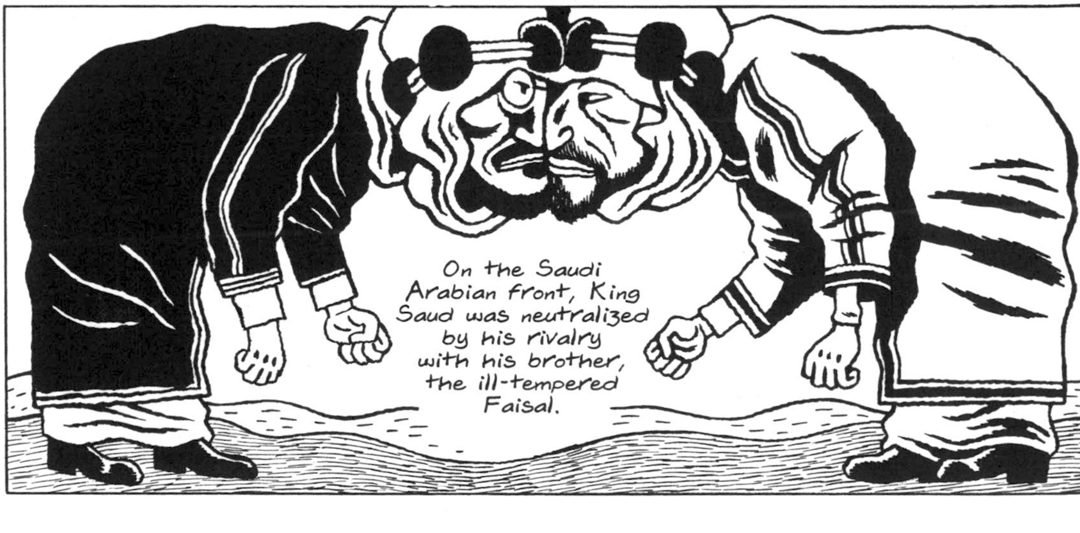
On the Saudi Arabian front, King Saud was neutralized by his rivalry with his brother, the ill-tempered Faisal.

Syria reclaimed its independence from the United Arab Republic which, in the end, proved far more Egyptian than Arab.

Syria accused Egypt of sacrificing the Palestinian cause for American aid.

September 1962 saw the death of Imam Ahmad, who had reigned over northern Yemen. Nasser's local disciples took the opportunity to seize power.

Anwar El Sadat, the president of the puppet Egyptian parliament and Nasser's close friend, called for immediate intervention.

The first Egyptian troops reached Yemen the next month.

They confronted the royalist rebellion, which refused to be defeated.

Nasser was forced to send ever more troops to quell this rebellion. By June 1967, 30% of the Egyptian army was engaged in Yemen.

Yemen was increasingly referred to as Egypt's Vietnam.

The rebels were actively supported by Saudi Arabia, which saw the Egyptian presence as a menace.

American oil companies and their Israeli contacts in Washington railed against Nasser's policies, their spokesman the indefatigable Kermit Roosevelt.

The U.S. Air Force was deployed on Saudi soil.

With Congress calling for escalation following Kennedy's assassination, relations between Cairo and Washington deteriorated.

Nasser strengthened his ties with Moscow.

He grew closer to the Ba'athists in power in Damascus.

He even indulged in the luxury of inviting to Cairo the former King Saud...

...who had been deposed by his brother Faisal in 1964.

On 30 May 1967, King Hussein of Jordan signed a treaty of military alliance with Egypt.

In 1964, he founded the PLO*, which was devoted to him.

* Palestinian Liberation Organization

And he used tensions with Israel to extend his influence.

So long as Israel exists, we can expect war at any moment.

The fact is that Zionists will not be satisfied with usurping Palestine.

They are preparing to found an empire of usurped territories running from the Nile to the Euphrates.

Nasser seemed to have won the Arab "Cold War".

And so he became the man for Washington's "cold warriors" to take down.

His victory would only last six days.

In 1956, Eisenhower forced the Israelis to retreat from Sinai and the Gaza Strip.

Israel then turned to its only unconditional ally, France, in order to obtain nuclear weapons.

Concerned by the Franco-Israeli agreement of 1961, the Kennedy administration secured permission to oversee the transfer, though most of the technology had already changed hands.

Presents Kennedy and then Johnson kept up official contact with Israel, thanks to advisor Myer Feldman.

Levi Eshkol, who became the Prime Minister of Israel in June 1963, sent alarmist messages about Egypt's ballistic missile programs.

The Pentagon remained skeptical about this threat.

An Israeli delegation led by Yitzhak Rabin conducted talks in Washington.

These were held in secret, as the U.S. wished to remain publicly neutral with regard to the Middle East.

These talks resulted in President Johnson's guaranteeing Israeli security, and the first shipments of arms there in 1965.

In 1967, a Pentagon assessment concluded that Israel was without a doubt strategically superior to its Arab neighbors.

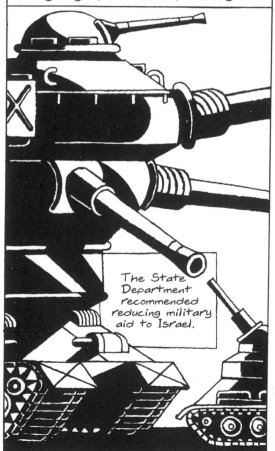

The State Department recommended reducing military aid to Israel.

For their part, Soviet experts stationed in Egypt tried in vain to convince Nasser there was no way his army could defeat the Israelis.

The Syrians accused him of cowardice, since his border with Israel was under U.N. protection.

He gave in to their blackmail and got the U.N. to withdraw its Blue Helmets.

A veritable hysteria for war took hold of the Arab media.

Israel planned a pre-emptive operation to neutralize the Egyptian threat.

On 21 May, under propaganda pressure from his Arab rivals, Nasser announced a blockade of the Straits of Tiran.

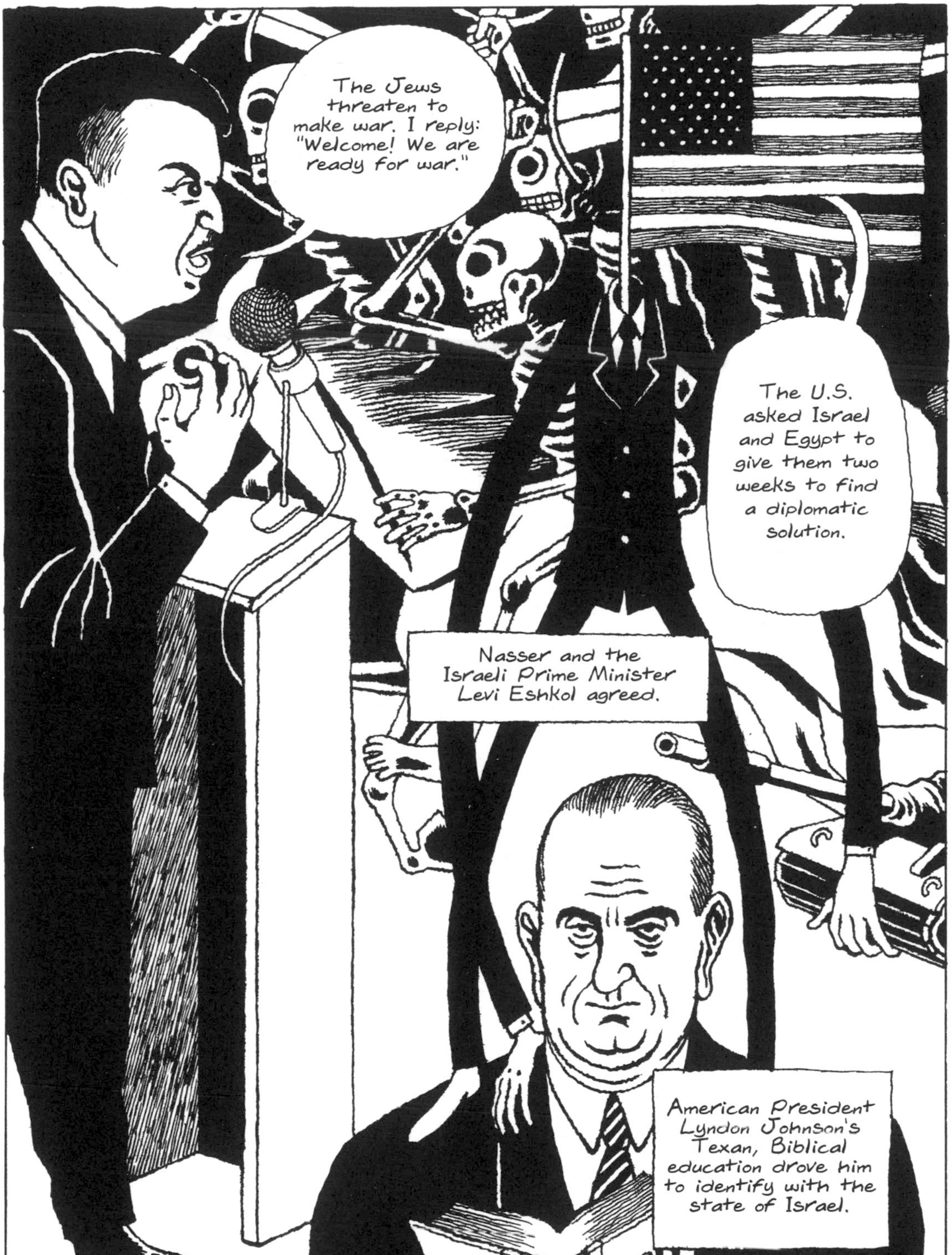
The Jews threaten to make war. I reply: "Welcome! We are ready for war."
The U.S. asked Israel and Egypt to give them two weeks to find a diplomatic solution.
Nasser and the Israeli Prime Minister Levi Eshkol agreed.
American President Lyndon Johnson's Texan, Biblical education drove him to identify with the state of Israel.

He saw the Israelis as a "frontier people" just like the Texans, who had fought the Mexicans in the 19th century.

Johnson told a story about saving dozens of survivors from the Nazi camps in 1945 during an operation codenamed "Texas".

In truth, he never took part in liberating the camps, and only intervened to allow two camp survivors to enter the U.S.

He was also anti-Communist on a gut level.

The installation of a Vietcong office in Cairo made him furious.

Still, he refused to see the Israeli emissaries who came to Washington after their new government was formed on 1 June.

Levi Eshkol sent me a message asking me to prevent another Holocaust.

In May, Jordan and Egypt had signed a defense pact, causing an uproar among Israeli generals that led to this change in government.

On 4 June 1967, the pre-emptive strike against Egypt was secretly approved.

On the morning of 5 June, the Israelis attacked, without warning their American allies.

The Israeli Air Force destroyed almost all the Egyptian planes, which were still on the ground.

21

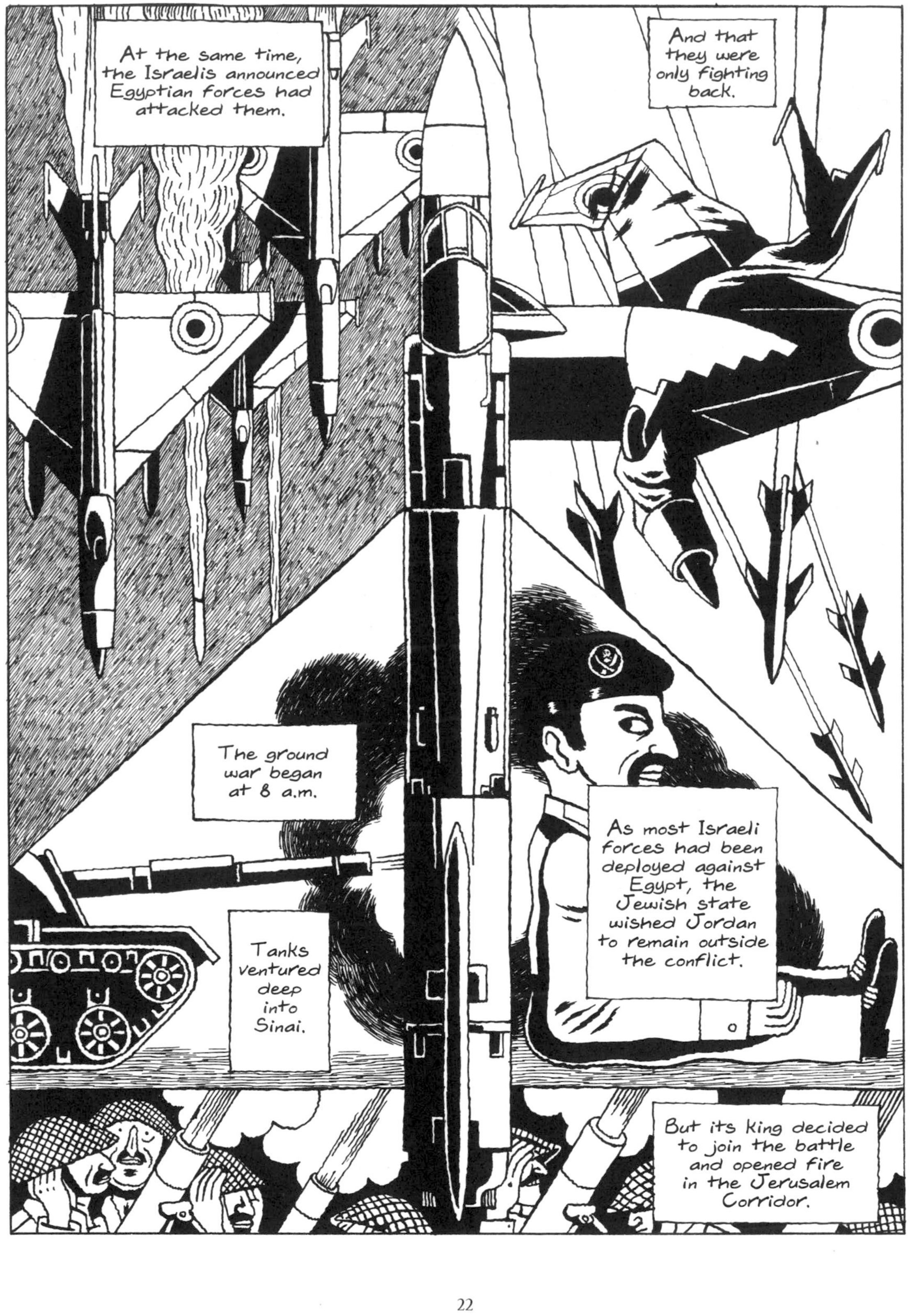
At the same time, the Israelis announced Egyptian forces had attacked them.
And that they were only fighting back.
The ground war began at 8 a.m.
Tanks ventured deep into Sinai.
As most Israeli forces had been deployed against Egypt, the Jewish state wished Jordan to remain outside the conflict.
But its king decided to join the battle and opened fire in the Jerusalem Corridor.

On their way back from their mission to Egypt, Israeli planes destroyed the air forces of Jordan, Syria, and Iraq, still on the ground.

The Arab armies were now deprived of all air support.

Surprised by the Israeli ground offensive, the Egyptian army found itself surrounded on the Sinai peninsula on the evening of 5 June.

On the Jordanian side, the fighting was very violent around Jerusalem.

Egypt had fed Jordan false reports to keep their ally from backing out on them.

They claimed to have fended off the Israelis, which redoubled the Jordanians' fighting spirit.

For their part, the Israelis made King Hussein endless offers of neutrality up till the last minute. These were all refused.

Nasser asked the Soviets to join the war on their side...

And replace all their destroyed planes.

The Soviets refused.

On the morning of 6 June, the two great powers were convinced Israel had already won the war.

The Soviets asked the Americans to stop the Israelis.

The U.S. refused, leaving the U.N. Security Council to settle the crisis.

Which gave Israel time to pursue its offensives.

It was in this context that Nasser, in order to explain the destruction of his air force, accused the U.S. of having taken part in the raids.

The U.S. government denied this, but in vain.

Protesters attacked their embassy in Tripoli, Libya.

On the morning of 6 June, the Egyptian army in Sinai received orders to fall back.

It was total chaos.

The soldiers were strafed by ground forces...

...and bombarded with napalm from the skies.

The Israelis took prisoners by the thousand.

In order not to slow their advance, some were let go, and others shot.

On the Jordanian front, the Israelis cut off East Jerusalem and raided the West Bank.

King Hussein asked the U.S. to stop Israel.

NO!

Johnson's administration refused, outraged by accusations of American belligerence that King Hussein had adopted from the Egyptians.

For Mossad had intercepted conversations between Nasser and Hussein, and made them public.

Conversations in which the two heads of state agreed on which accusations to hurl at the Americans.

Cairo then severed diplomatic relations with Washington, D.C.

Algiers, Damascus, Sana'a, Khartoum, and Baghdad followed.

The American embassies were attacked again, and their nationals evacuated.

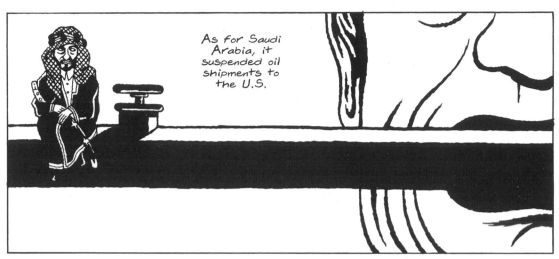

As for Saudi Arabia, it suspended oil shipments to the U.S.

However, both the U.S. and the U.S.S.R. were advocating a ceasefire.

Jordan agreed, but Egypt required that any agreement respect the borders of 5 June.

On 7 June, the Egyptian High Command canceled the previous day's order to retreat.

Which only increased the confusion.

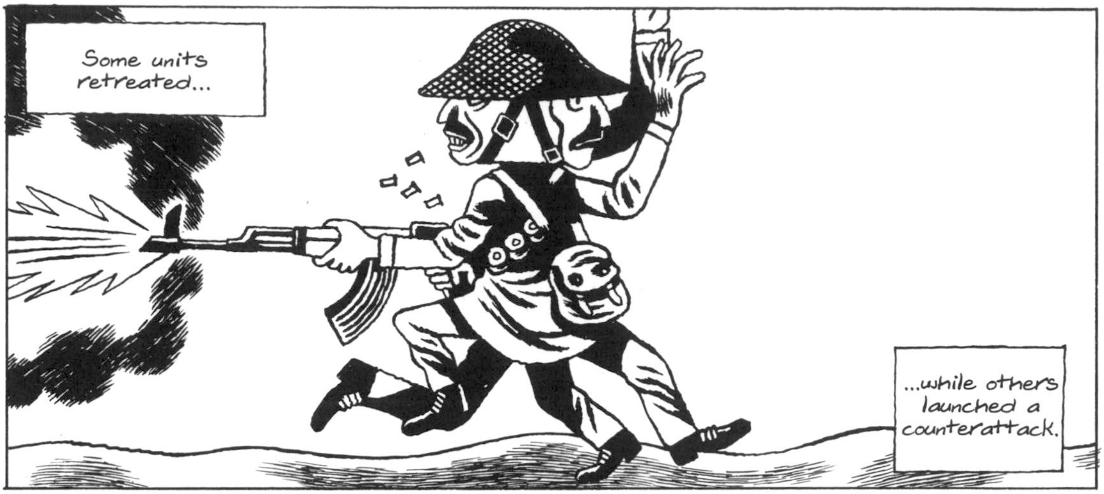
Some units retreated...
...while others launched a counterattack.

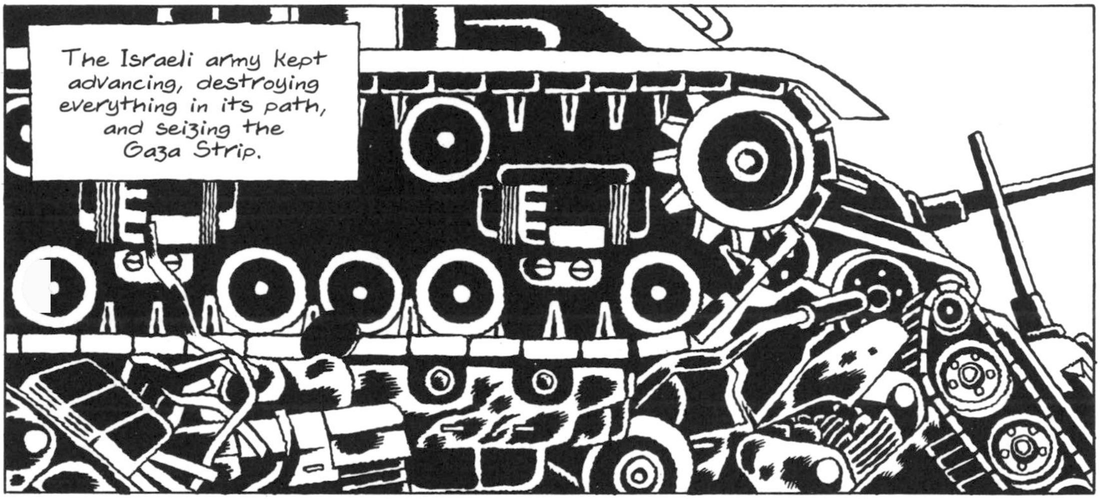
The Israeli army kept advancing, destroying everything in its path, and seizing the Gaza Strip.

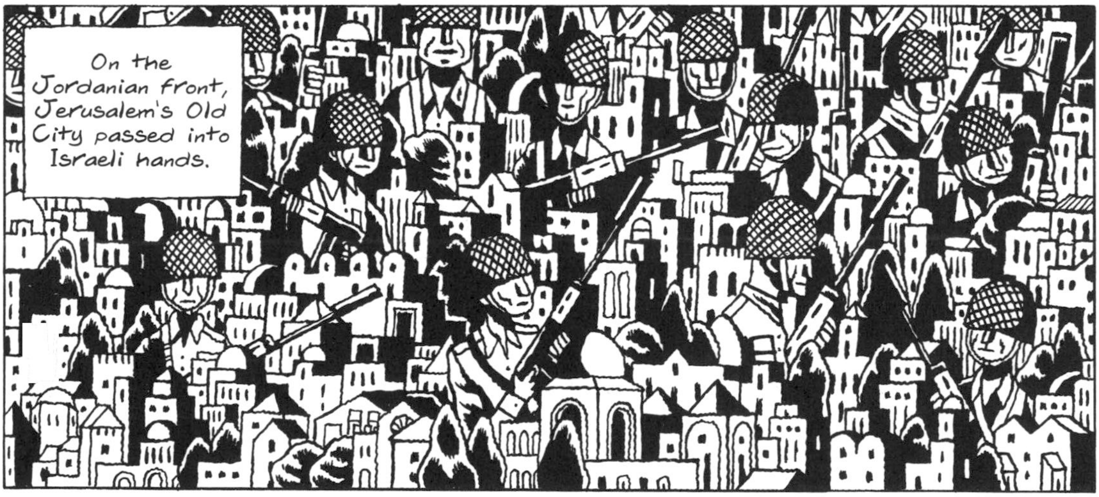
On the Jordanian front, Jerusalem's Old City passed into Israeli hands.

The Israeli Defense Forces (I.D.F.) reached the Wailing Wall.

First the Jordanians lost the city, and then their army collapsed, retreating over the bridges on the Jordan River.

On 8 June, the Israeli army reached the Suez Canal.

The U.S.S.R. wanted peace at any price, and this time, Egypt agreed to an unconditional ceasefire.

Moscow delivered an ultimatum to Israel: stop fighting, or we will intervene.

On 9 June, Nasser admitted his responsibility for the defeat...

I am ready to bear the whole responsibility... I have decided to give up completely and finally every official post and every political role...

...but continued to accuse the U.S.

He handed in not only his own resignation, but those of the entire political and military leadership.

A wave of people filled the streets of Cairo begging him to stay in power.

Which Nasser agreed to do... while standing by the resignation of other officials.

Given free rein, the Israelis decided to settle their accounts with the Syrians.

The Golan Heights had been subjected to intense bombardment in the preceding days.

The Syrians, well-entrenched, defended themselves doggedly, slowing the Israeli advance.

But certain I.D.F. units reached the plateau by day's end.

As the U.N. ceasefire was soon to be enforced, the Israelis rushed the plateau.

To hasten the U.N.'s actions, the Syrian government announced the main Golani town, Quneitra, had fallen before it actually had.

This announcement caused the Syrian forces to scatter in disarray.

The Syrian authorities preferred to withdraw from Golan and protect Damascus.

On 10 June, the war officially ended.

The ceasefire was announced toward the end of the afternoon, but the Israelis continued their advance.

It lasted another two days...

...till Golan was entirely occupied.

6 Between Two Wars

Throughout the Arab world, the U.S. found themselves accused of having directly aided the Israeli offensive of 1967.

U.S. embassies burned...

...as did their schools and cultural centers.

The U.S.S.R. and (with the exception of Romania) the Soviet bloc...

...severed diplomatic relations with Israel.

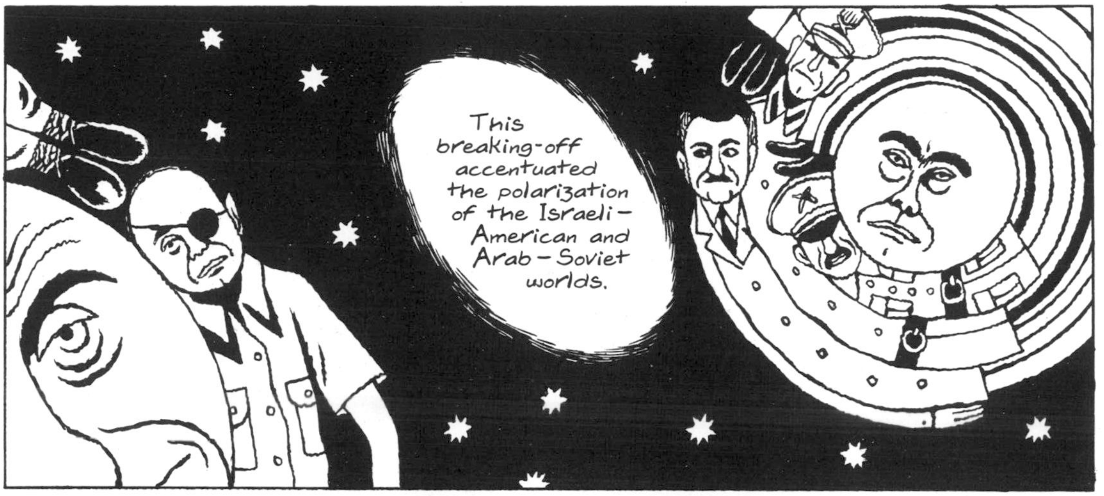
This breaking-off accentuated the polarization of the Israeli–American and Arab–Soviet worlds.

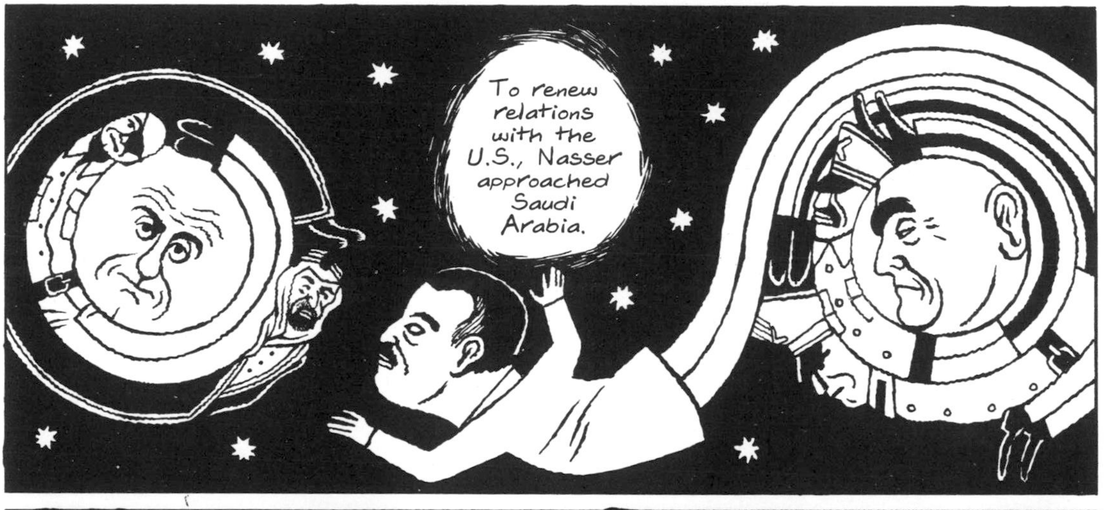
To renew relations with the U.S., Nasser approached Saudi Arabia.

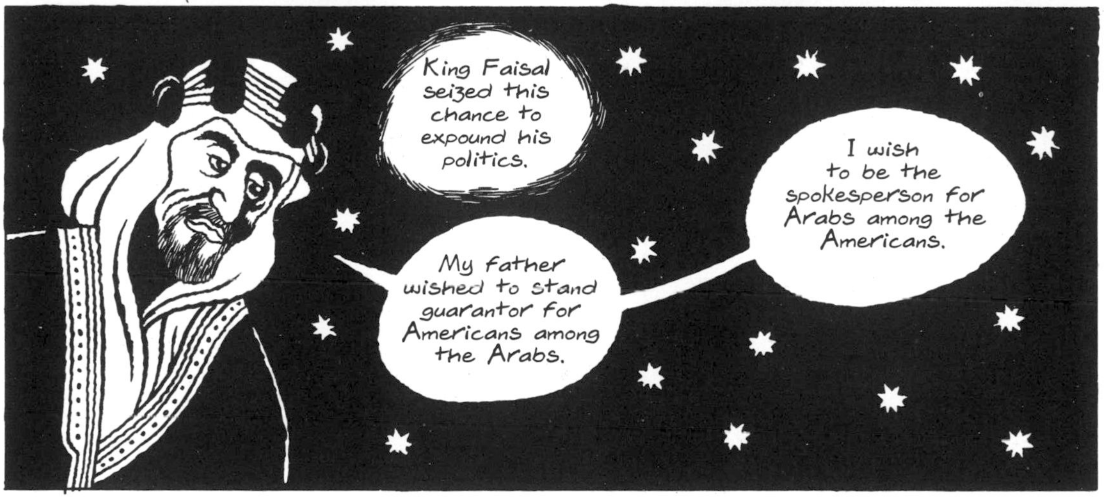
King Faisal seized this chance to expound his politics.
I wish to be the spokesperson for Arabs among the Americans.
My father wished to stand guarantor for Americans among the Arabs.

Fresh from their victories, the Israelis emptied the Jordan Valley and the Golan Heights of 90% of their people, forbidding them to return.

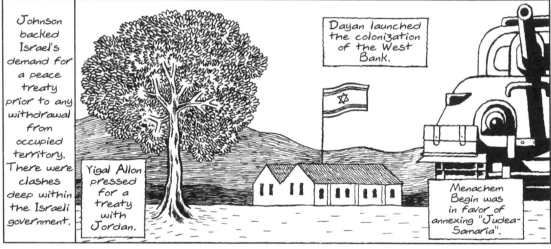

Johnson backed Israel's demand for a peace treaty prior to any withdrawal from occupied territory. There were clashes deep within the Israeli government.

Yigal Allon pressed for a treaty with Jordan.

Dayan launched the colonization of the West Bank.

Menachem Begin was in favor of annexing "Judea-Samaria".

Inter-Arab escalation ensued.

No peace with Israel.

No recognition of Israel.

No negotiations with Israel.

At the 1967 Arab League Summit in Khartoum, Syria obtained unanimity for its "Three No's".

At the same time, Israel saw its position reinforced with a very favorable status quo.

In November 1967, the U.S. voted for U.N. Security Council Resolution 242, which in French stipulated Israeli withdrawal from "the" territories occupied in the recent conflict.

But in the English version, the definite article was omitted ("withdrawal of Israeli forces from territories occupied"), and the Israeli interpretation of a conditional withdrawal won out.

French and English are the two working languages of the U.N., and are of equal legal force.

A "War of Attrition" unfolded along the Suez Canal from March 1969 through August 1970.

While Rogers, the newly elected President Nixon's Secretary of State, tried to find a peaceful solution...

...the Pentagon and Security Advisor Kissinger encouraged Israel to bomb Egypt heavily and make Nasser fold.

Kissinger believed Egypt must get nothing from Israel until it broke off relations with the U.S.S.R.

The Arab leaders will come to us, in the end.

In August 1970, Israel and Egypt signed a ceasefire under the aegis of the U.N.

An accord between Israel and Jordan was taking shape.

But the Palestinian commandos who had set up opposition forces in Jordan had to be reckoned with.

Clashes broke out with the army.

Western planes were hijacked to an airport in Jordan.

King Hussein was forced to answer the challenge, resulting in "Black September".

The U.S. deployed the 6th Fleet to the Mediterranean.

The Jordanian army gave the Palestinians no quarter.

Israel declared itself ready to intervene and save King Hussein's reign.

The Syrians sent tanks to help the Palestinians, but these were destroyed by the Jordanian air force.

The ailing Nasser used his last ounce of strength to get a ceasefire between Jordan and Palestine...

...dying shortly after it was announced.

The U.S. marched to victory alongside the Jordanians and the Israelis.

Sadat succeeded Nasser in Egypt, while Hafez el-Assad came to power in Syria.

In 1971, the Shah was celebrating 2,500 years of Iranian monarchy in Persepolis. He had openly sided with Israel during these conflicts.

Re-elected in 1972, Nixon refused Israel nothing. Dayan and his military hierarchy were convinced of their omnipotence.

However, Sadat was secretly planning a coordinated strike with Syria.

On 6 October 1973 — on Yom Kippur, the Jewish holy day, and during the Islamic month of Ramadan — Egyptian and Syrian armies broke through Israeli lines.

Despite successful counteroffensives in the Sinai Peninsula and the Golan Heights, the shock to the Jewish state was enormous.

Sadat, whose forces had crossed the Suez Canal, hoped that his Third Army would be able to continue his attack.

On 12 October, Nixon called for a ceasefire. When the Egyptians refused, he cited this as a reason to organize a military air bridge to help Israel.

The Soviets did the same, supplying the Arab armies with weapons and ammunition.

On 16 October, the Israeli army established a bridgehead on the West Bank of the Suez Canal. Meanwhile, on the Syrian front, they were nearing Damascus.

This was too much for King Faisal, who used oil as a weapon.

He decided to embargo all oil to the U.S. Other oil-producing countries soon followed suit.

He demanded that an accord be signed stipulating an Israeli withdrawal to the 1967 borders.

Even if the U.S. only depended on Saudi oil for 4% of its consumption, the cost rose from 4 billion to 24 billion dollars in 1974.

Under the Shah, Iran profited from the rise in oil prices and refused to join the Arab embargo.

On 22 October, the U.N. Security Council called for an immediate ceasefire, which Israel refused.

This was because the Israeli army hoped to crush Egypt's Third Army, which it had surrounded in the Sinai Desert.

The U.S.S.R. put its troops on a state of alert. There was talk of a nuclear threat. Under American pressure, Israel gave in.

The war lasted 18 days... three times as long as in 1967.

In its wake, the West was divided between the U.S., which was identified with Israel, and Europe and Japan, which depended greatly on Arab oil.

Henry Kissinger crisscrossed the Middle East in an effort to impose a simple principle:

There was no war the Arabs could win in that region...

...not even with Soviet help.

There was no hope of peace without American backing.

During the negotiations, he divided Sinai and the Golan Heights into two separate issues, obtaining two separate withdrawal accords from Israel.

In doing so, he broke the common Egyptian-Syrian front of 1973...

...and restored the privileged axis between Washington and Riyadh.

Kissinger left the U.S.S.R. out of the diplomatic game, thus meting out revenge for the American defeat in Vietnam on the Middle East.

To Israel, he maintained that limited concessions allowed them to cede nothing essential.

To the Arabs, he asserted that the accords were a first step toward settling the conflicts as a whole.

Thus did peace, instead of drawing nearer, drift ever further away.

7 1979

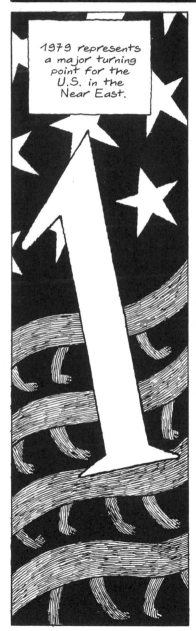

1979 represents a major turning point for the U.S. in the Near East.

Stricken by "Vietnam syndrome", America elected an obscure Democrat from Georgia in 1976: Jimmy Carter.

Deeply religious, he wanted a clean break with the moral compromises of his Republican predecessors, Nixon and Ford.

He was revolted by Kissinger's avowed political cynicism, and support for pro-Western dictatorships.

He advocated reconciliation between the "sons of Abraham": Israel and the Arab world.

President Sadat's visit to Jerusalem in 1977 paved the way.

In Israel, Menachem Begin's unyielding right-wing government had come to power.

It denied the existence of a Palestinian people...

...but was ready to make concessions to Egypt to reinforce the occupation of the West Bank, that "Judea-Samaria", he believed, was part of "Greater Israel".

In 1978, Carter hosted Begin and Sadat at Camp David for closed-door negotiations.

He himself shuttled between the two parties.

With great effort, he secured peace accords that won Sadat and Begin the Nobel Peace Prize.

But the nightmare that was 1979 was only just beginning.

The Iranian Revolution

In 1953, the religious hierarchy of the Ayatollahs had taken up the fight against the "Communist threat" of Mossadegh, favoring the pro-American coup d'état that installed the Shah.

But the ambitious Ruhollah Khomeini distinguished himself from the other high leaders by condemning the Shah's politics and the privileges granted the regime's American advisors.

Exiled to Iraq in 1965, Khomeini cultivated a mixture of nationalism and religious conservatism that would cause an opposition movement to crystallize around him against the Shah's dictatorship.

Demonstrations in the street followed one after another in a murderous, relentless cycle in 1978.

Each protest fed on "martyrs" from the one before.

Each was more violent than the last.

In Iraq, the Shi'a ferment began to worry Saddam Hussein.

And so he sought to rid himself of Khomeini.

France under Valéry Giscard d'Estaing was deeply involved both economically and militarily with Iraq, and took in the Iranian religious leader.

The Ayatollah respected his duty to formal reserve.

But his impassioned recordings spread throughout Iran.

In Tehran, demonstrations turned against the symbols of "Western decadence".

On 23 October 1978, bars, hotels, movie theaters, and restaurants were vandalized.

The mostazafin, as the Islamic revolution called the poorest class, became the "wretched of the earth" in the new anti-Imperialist rhetoric.

Certain high-ranking army officials urged the Shah to more drastic repression.

The Shah hesitated.

The country, his regime, and his "fourth army of the world" collapsed.

The Shah decided to get out, and suddenly fled the country.

On 1 February 1979, Ayatollah Khomeini returned to Tehran, where he was welcomed by a human tide of several million people.

On 11 February, the first Islamic revolution in history triumphed in Iran, the "gendarme of the Gulf".

The powerful Israeli embassy was occupied, turned into an embassy for Palestine...

...and handed over to Yasser Arafat's representative in Tehran.

In the Muslim world, an entire generation of militant anti-imperialists, once the staunchest Marxists, became the most radical Muslims.

The Israeli-Arab Peace

Abandoned by his former allies, the Shah took refuge in Egypt.

The hospitality Sadat extended him made matters worse when he was publicly accused of treason for negotiating with the Zionist enemy.

In Khomeini's rhetoric, the "Great Satan" of America fed and protected the "Little Satan" of Israel, which was doomed to disappear with the inevitable triumph of Islam.

Things went downhill for Sadat when Begin refused to recognize any form of Palestinian national rights.

The residents of the West Bank were "individuals" with no collective rights.

The colonization of "Judea-Samaria" continued without let-up.

Jimmy Carter managed to "midwife" two accords at Camp David: the first, a global accord on the end of the occupation of the West Bank and the Gaza Strip.

The second, a limited accord on the Israeli-Egyptian conflict.

Begin's systematic blocking led to the first accord being buried. Only the Israeli-Egyptian peace remained.

Israel had carried off a threefold victory.

A symbolic one, because of the formal recognition and establishment of diplomatic relations with Egypt.

A strategic one, because Israel's most formidable foe was thus neutralized.

And a political one, with the break-up of the Arab side.

Egypt received substantial American aid.

Which allowed it to achieve "de-Nasserization", to the benefit of the nouveau riche, who were both pro-West and Islamist-friendly.

Sinai was returned to Egypt in three phases from 1979 to 1982.

But Egypt was excluded from the Arab League.

Jimmy Carter had to be satisfied with a partial peace that privileged Israel, marginalized Egypt, and confirmed "hawks" on all sides in their opinions.

Black November

No sooner was it validated by a referendum than the Islamic Republic tore itself apart in factional struggles.

Ayatollah Khomeini showed his true colors.

His desire to become the supreme leader of a theocratic regime became clear.

Summary executions followed one after another.

Ayatollah Khalkhali castigated clemency as anti-revolutionary.

Differences deepened.

Defenders of order against self-proclaimed militias.

Persian nationalists against defenders of Kurds or Arabs.

Uncompromising purifiers against recyclers of executives from the previous regime.

Partisans of socialism crossbred with Islamism against "bazaris" in favor of economic liberalism.

Escalation ensued. That summer, each side accused the other of being in the pockets of foreigners.

On 4 November, the pro-Khomeini "Student followers of the Imam's Line" attacked the U.S. Embassy, which they called a "nest of spies".

The students paraded the 66 American hostages.

The overt crises allowed Khomeini's followers to silence all domestic dissidence. Deemed too liberal, Prime Minister Mehdi Bazargan was forced to resign.

Jimmy Carter froze Iranian assets in the U.S. and suspended all oil imports from Iran.

An American military operation to free the hostages failed in the Iranian desert after two helicopters crashed.

In July 1980, Iraqi attacks against Iran eventually turned into the first Gulf War.

Ensuing negotiations to free the hostages were mediated by Algeria before the American presidential elections in November.

The Republican camp bypassed the Democrats, launching their own parallel negotiations.

These raised the stakes and delayed the hostages' release.

Tehran announced their release ten minutes after Reagan's nomination was announced.

Massacre in Mecca

On 20 November 1979, a group of millenarian insurgents seized the Grand Mosque in Mecca.

Responding to this sacrilege, Saudi authorities imposed a blackout and, after pitched combat, took back the mosque with the help of French commandos.

But false rumors spread like wildfire that American forces had occupied Islam's holiest site.

Thousands of protesters took the American embassy in Islamabad by storm. It took the Pakistani army to clear them out.

Similar attacks occurred in Turkey, Bangladesh, Kuwait, and Libya.

Invasion of Afghanistan

Since 1978, Afghanistan has been run by the local Communist party, with Moscow's support.

The U.S.S.R. supplied military support against the various Islamist movements.

But Russia's political advisors had, above all, to appease conflicts among implacable factions at the heart of the Afghan Communist Party.

These grew worse in the fall of 1979, and on 27 December, the Red Army directly intervened to prevent the regime's collapse.

Soviet commandos took out the master of Kabul, Hafizullah Amin, replacing him with their puppet: Babrak Karmal.

The U.S.S.R. seized control of the country's main axes.

But the invasion of the "infidels" led to an uprising of Afghan insurgents in the name of jihad.

The U.S. condemned the show of force, but security advisor Zbigniew Brzezinski recommended letting the Soviets become embroiled in uncontrollable terrain.

A way of taking revenge for the defeat in Vietnam, and wearing out the U.S.S.R., which was locked into a massive arms race.

Washington decided to wage a war by proxy.

The Pakistani secret service controlled training camps by the border...

...and the Saudi services financed the revolt thanks to funds from the CIA.

One such Saudi, seduced by the epic of the Afghan jihad, settled in Pakistan and raised funds in the Gulf to support the cause.

He soon attained a prestige equal to his generosity.

8 Lebanon 1982 – 1984

In 1975, the civil war that had been brewing in Lebanon broke out between Christians and the Palestinian refugees and their allies.

The Syrian military intervened in 1976, but it could not stop the violence.

This ranged from the murder of individuals to massacres of entire communities.

In 1978, it was the Israelis' turn to intervene and protect the cities in the north of the country from P.L.O. attacks.

The I.D.F. withdrew after a few weeks.

Ronald Reagan and his administration were Israel's lasting allies.

The Jewish state was considered an advance bastion of the free world against the U.S.S.R.'s Arab allies.

Israel was encouraged to harass Syria and the P.L.O. to weaken Moscow's influence in the region.

Peace for Galilee

On either side of the Israel–Lebanon border, Israelis and Palestinian refugees in Lebanon turned to dueling with artillery.

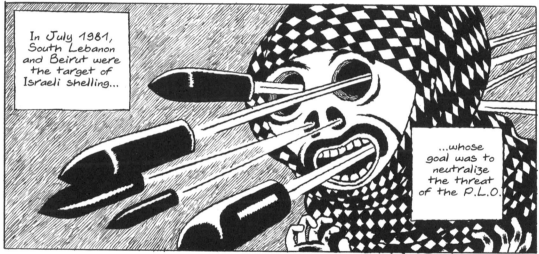

In July 1981, South Lebanon and Beirut were the target of Israeli shelling...

...whose goal was to neutralize the threat of the P.L.O.

The U.S. indirectly brokered a ceasefire between the P.L.O. and Israel...

...since the Americans did not want to negotiate directly with Yasser Arafat's organization.

This armed truce lasted almost a year.

On 3 June 1982, the Israeli ambassador in London was the target of an attack by Abu Nidal's group.

Abu Nidal was a P.L.O. dissident whom Arafat had condemned to death.

But Begin saw this attack as a violation of the ceasefire.

On 4 June, the Israeli air force bombed Palestinian camps in West Beirut.

South Lebanon was bombarded by land, sea, and air.

Palestinian artillery fired back on Upper Galilee.

Begin used the shelling to justify intervention on Lebanese soil to Reagan.

For seven hours now, 23 of our cities in Galilee have been under bombardment from artillery supplied by the U.S.S.R. and Katyusha rockets from P.L.O. terrorists. This shelling is aimed exclusively at civilian populations...

The bloodthirsty enemy is at our door. Do we not have an inherent right to self-defense?

The army has received orders to make the terrorists retreat a distance of 25 miles to the north.

We do not covet a single inch of Lebanese soil. We wish to sign a peace treaty with a free and independent Lebanon that retains its territorial integrity.

The U.S. diplomatically backed this invasion, and the red telephone rang off the hook between Reagan and Brezhnev.

This isn't our fight.

We'll do all we can to stop Israel.

For its part, the U.S.S.R. condemned the invasion, but made no threats.

...

Saudi Arabia felt abandoned by the most pro-Israeli American administration since the war.

...

It turned toward another member of the Western camp: France.

U.S. Secretary of State Alexander Haig fought for the idea of a buffer zone to ensure the safety of Israel's northern border.

In Lebanon, Israelis reached the gates of Beirut after decimating the Syrian air force.

The Syrians withdrew from the conflict, leaving the Palestinians and the Israelis face to face. Only a contingent of 3,500 men remained in West Beirut.

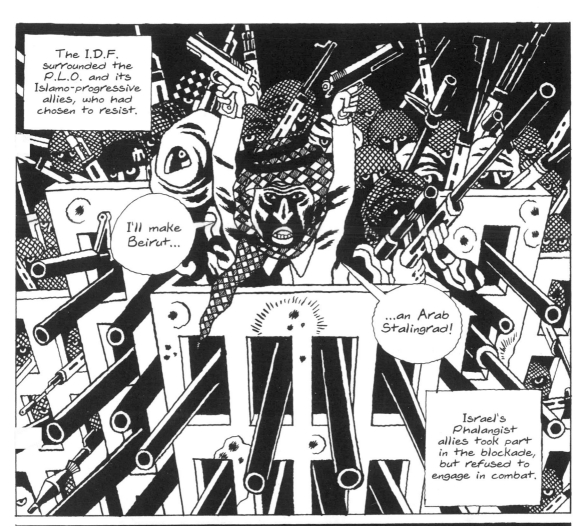

The I.D.F. surrounded the P.L.O. and its Islamo-progressive allies, who had chosen to resist.

I'll make Beirut...

...an Arab Stalingrad!

Israel's Phalangist allies took part in the blockade, but refused to engage in combat.

To French Minister of Foreign Affairs Claude Cheysson, Haig proposed the creation of a Saudi-Kuwaiti-Franco-American contact group on Lebanon.

Cheysson paid a visit to President François Mitterrand at his retreat in Latche.

I've made it clear to Haig that an essential element is missing from all this: the fate of the Palestinians.

He did not greet this remark with enthusiasm.

That same day in Washington, the Israeli and French ambassadors met.

Some intermediary step must come before the Israeli retreat from Lebanon...

...and we must first set up a multinational peacekeeping force.

The Habib Plan

On 22 June 1982, the Palestinians sent the French Embassy in Lebanon the following propositions:

Withdrawal of Palestinian troops from West Beirut, surrender of heavy artillery, and regrouping into four refugee camps.

The Lebanese army could be deployed along the Palestinian positions.

The Israelis would have to fall back 10 km from Beirut.

The Palestinian propositions were conveyed to Reagan's new emissary Philip Habib, who had coordinated the ceasefire in South Lebanon in 1981.

The U.S. refused these propositions. Like Israel, they wanted the P.L.O. to surrender.

Attempting to settle the conflict turned into a delicate diplomatic ballet.

One of the heated moments was Alexander Haig's resignation, and his replacement by George Shultz.

French diplomats lent their good offices to talks between the Palestinians and the U.S.

The entire American strategy was to block the French initiative.

America demanded the Palestinian fighters disarm and leave Lebanon.

On 26 June at the U.N. Security Council, 14 members voted in favor of the French draft resolution, but the Americans vetoed it.

To force an agreement, the U.S. spread false news...

...claiming that the P.L.O. had agreed to evacuate 5,000 combatants, and that Marines were landing in Lebanon.

For its part, the Israeli army tightened its stranglehold on West Beirut, cutting off water and electricity, as well as starting a food blockade.

On 4 August, the Israelis launched an attack on Beirut, but the Palestinians resisted fiercely.

A fuel-air bomb demolished an apartment building where the IDF believed Arafat was hiding.

Israeli leaders were obsessed with killing Arafat.

That was why he was always switching hideouts.

On 10 August, the Israelis launched another attack, without success.

Israel accepted the Habib Plan...

...even as their armies shelled Beirut.

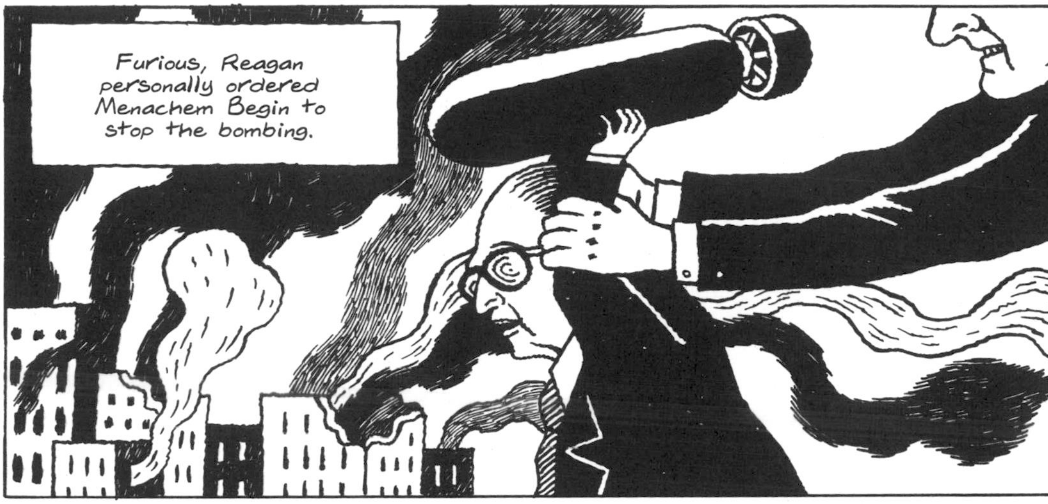
Furious, Reagan personally ordered Menachem Begin to stop the bombing.

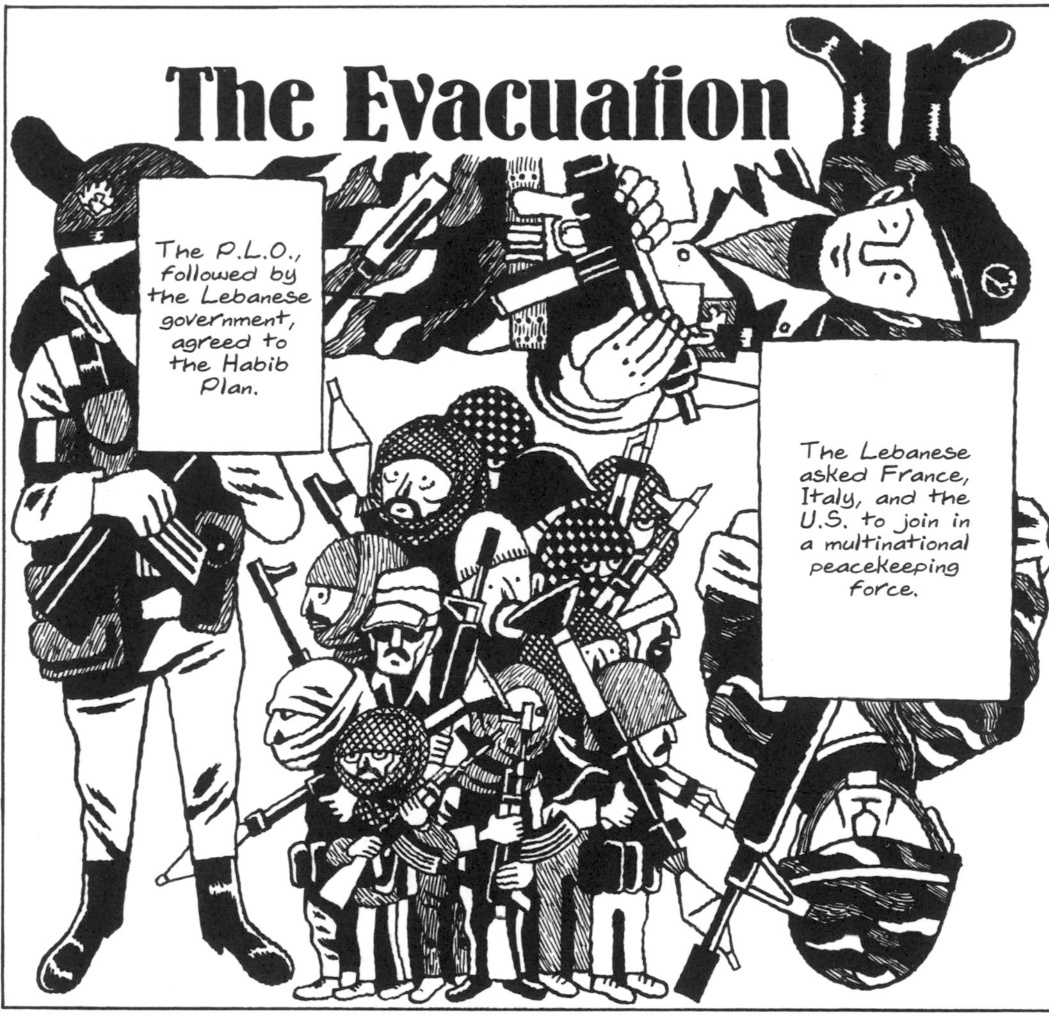
The Evacuation
The P.L.O., followed by the Lebanese government, agreed to the Habib Plan.
The Lebanese asked France, Italy, and the U.S. to join in a multinational peacekeeping force.

The various contingents made their landing from 21 to 25 August. After a few skirmishes with the Israeli army, the evacuation proceeded smoothly.

More than 14,000 Fedayeens left Beirut.

In the eastern part of the town, under Israeli control, Bachir Gemayel was elected president of the republic.

The election
of a pro-
Western
president
went hand
in hand
with the
Israeli army's
efforts.

On 30
August,
Arafat
left Beirut,
escorted by
legionnaires
and the
French
ambassador.

The election of
Gemayel and the
evacuation of the
Palestinians tolled
a defeat for the
"Islamo-progressives".

A defeat
both military and
political.

Furious at seeing Arafat escape, Ariel Sharon rounded on Mitterrand and let him have it.

By giving the P.L.O., an organization of terrorists and murderers, this kind of encouragement, President Mitterrand has prolonged this war.

The Reagan Plan

On 1 September, Ronald Reagan delivered a speech intended to relaunch the Palestinian track from the Camp David accords.

He called for a settlement freeze in the West Bank and the Gaza Strip...

...the retreat of the I.D.F. from territories occupied in 1967...

...and the creation of a self-governing Palestinian authority in association with Jordan.

Israel rejected the Reagan Plan.

On 3 September, the Israeli army, in violation of the Habib Plan, advanced toward the Sabra and Shatila Palestinian refugee camps.

This troop movement provoked no reaction from Western forces.

The U.S. were eager to leave Beirut as soon as possible.

From Tunisia, where he had taken refuge, Arafat asked France to protect Lebanon's civilian population.

And the Israeli army edged ever closer to the camps.

The I.D.F. claimed the Palestinian Fedayeen and Lebanese militia remained hidden in south Beirut, and threatened to flush them out by force.

On 10 September, American troops from the multinational force left Lebanon.

The Italians left on the 11th and the French on the 13th.

On 14 September, a bomb devastated the seat of the Phalange Party. Among the victims was President Gemayel.

The next day, the Israeli army launched an attack on West Beirut, where members of "Islamo-progressive" militias were still putting up resistance.

On the night of the 16th, Phalangist militia penetrated the Sabra and Shatila camps, killing civilians.

When the massacre was discovered, 400,000 Israelis protested in Tel-Aviv, calling the position of Sharon and Begin into question.

The government investigative committee found Israel indirectly responsible, and Sharon personally responsible.

Return to Beirut

The UN called for military protection of the civilian population in Beirut. Washington pushed for a new multinational force, free from a UN mandate.

This time, the British joined the French, the Americans, and the Italians.

On 21 September, Amine Gemayel, Bachir's older brother, was elected president by the Lebanese parliament.

The first attacks on the contingents of the multinational force occurred in February 1983. The "Islamic Jihad" movement claimed responsibility.

Diplomats made the connection between the "Islamic Jihad" and the self-proclaimed Islamic Republic in Baalbek.

This republic, backed and financed by the Iranians, gathered radical Shi'a movements.

The most significant among them was a faction of the Amal movement called Islamic Amal.

But it was the party of God, or "Hezbollah", that stood out in the Lebanese theater.

On 18 April, while in a meeting with his team, the CIA's Near East director was killed when an explosion destroyed the U.S. Embassy.

Islamic Jihad claimed responsibility for the attack and issued a stamp commemorating it.

The attack had the effect of accelerating negotiations between Israel and Lebanon under the aegis of the Reagan administration.

The treaty provided for a "security belt" in South Lebanon, to be patrolled by two Lebanese army brigades. The I.D.F. retained a "right of inspection".

The withdrawal of Israeli forces was dependent on an equal and opposite withdrawal of Syrian forces.

That was when the Druze Progressive Socialist Party, allied with Syria, drove the Lebanese army back from the Chouf District.

The Druzes advanced all the way to Souk El Gharb, the gateway to Beirut. There, on 11 September, American artillery intervened on behalf of the Lebanese army and drove back the P.S.P. militia.

The U.S. sent over more troops and warships.

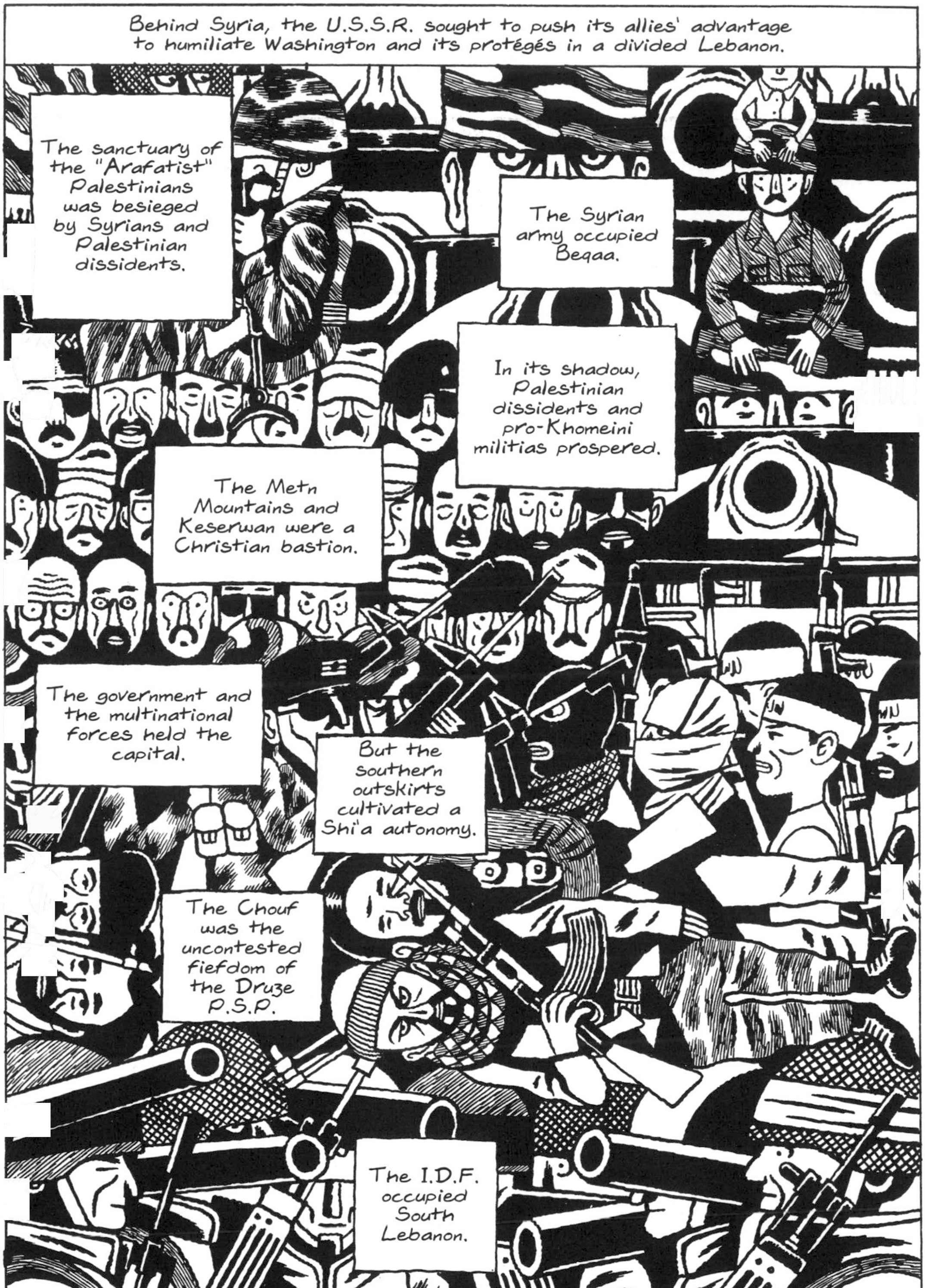
Behind Syria, the U.S.S.R. sought to push its allies' advantage to humiliate Washington and its protégés in a divided Lebanon.
The sanctuary of the "Arafatist" Palestinians was besieged by Syrians and Palestinian dissidents.
The Syrian army occupied Beqaa.
In its shadow, Palestinian dissidents and pro-Khomeini militias prospered.
The Metn Mountains and Keserwan were a Christian bastion.
The government and the multinational forces held the capital.
But the southern outskirts cultivated a Shi'a autonomy.
The Chouf was the uncontested fiefdom of the Druze P.S.P.
The I.D.F. occupied South Lebanon.

On 23 October, suicide bombers crashed explosive-rigged trucks into two buildings: the French paratrooper Drakkar outpost...

... and the barracks of the American Marines.

On 26 October, Vice-President George Bush went to Beirut. Massive American retaliation was expected.

Instead, American forces were sent to Grenada to topple the pro-Cuban regime.

On 3 December, Syrian batteries fired on American planes on a reconnaissance mission over the Chouf.

The next day, bombers pounded the Syrian positions.

In Beirut, the multinational force was the target of regular attacks.

Enemies of the Lebanese regime were trying to force the contingents from their country.

Instead, the Lebanese army asked the multinational force to help them drive out the Amal Shi'as from south Beirut.

The U.S. agreed, but the other governments refused.

On 3 February 1984, the Lebanese army launched a solo attack on the Amal positions, but the Sixth Brigade, composed of Shi'a soldiers, changed sides.

Faced with the collapse of the Lebanese army, the British, Italian, and American contingents got back on their ships. Reagan announced that the contingent had been redeployed "offshore".

On 5 March 1984, Amine Gemayel found himself forced to repeal the Israeli-Lebanese peace agreement regarding South Lebanon.

It was a failure for advocates of the new Cold War, who surrounded Ronald Reagan.

The "Reagan Plan" was stillborn, as Likud refused any and all concessions on Palestinian rights.

The CIA and the Marines had suffered very heavy losses, and the U.S. could not prevent the disbanding of the Lebanese army.

Plans for a projected reconstruction of the region around an Israeli-Lebanese axis fell apart in the face of Syria's return in force.

About the Author

Jean-Pierre Filiu, a historian and an arabist, is professor at Sciences Po, Paris School of International Affairs (PSIA). After an extensive career in the Middle East, first with NGOs, then as a diplomat, he has held visiting professorships both at Columbia (New York) and at Georgetown (Washington). His *Apocalypse in Islam* (University of California Press, 2011) was awarded the main prize by the French History Convention. His works and articles about contemporary Islam have been published in a dozen languages. His most recent book is *Arab Revolution: Ten Lessons from the Democratic Uprising* (Hurst, London and Oxford University Press, New York).

About the Author/Artist

David B. is the Eisner Award-nominated artist behind *Epileptic*, an autobiographical story widely considered a masterpiece of the graphic-novel medium. A founding member of the revolutionary French independent publisher L'Association, he is regarded as a giant among Bandes Dessinées artists. His many prizes include the Prix de Cheverny (2007), the Ignatz Award for Outstanding Artist (2005), and the top prizes for Comics Writing (2002) and Best Comic Book (1998, 2004) at the Angoulême International Comics Festival. His *Black Paths* – the extraordinary story of the Dadaist poet Gabriele d'Annunzio – was published by SelfMadeHero in 2011.